AF255718

GET YOUR SH*T TOGETHER

GOODBYE Fear, Resentment, and Failure HELLO Healing, Freedom, and Empowerment

By Alesia Lester-Braimah

A Note from Alesia 

I am BACK! As promised, I could never go on this journey
alone, so this book is to spread unspeakable joy to all of
you. I have grown tremendously since my last book titled
"Life Behind the Chair" by Alesia Lester. While of course
life has not always been easy, the healing is immeasurable.
After losing my mother to Covid in June of 2021, I knew
I would be forever changed. She taught me the meaning
of unconditional love and to never kiss anyone's ass, I am
great at both. She was phenomenal. I dedicate this book to
you momma, you planted a seed of confidence in me that
will grow forever, rest well "girlfriend."

Table of Contents

Introduction

For those that know me, it is safe to say that I never imagined my life at the point that it is now. I am married with an amazing, blended family and two new toddlers that keep me on my toes daily. I wake up each day preparing breakfast, packing lunch bags, and dropping tiny people off at school. I come home, and make coffee for my husband and me as we head into our home office to work. We have also been blessed with four grandchildren that light up our world. If 10 years ago, someone would have asked if I were interested in this role, I would have declined, only because I was single-minded meaning I only thought as a single woman with one child, our needs were minimal, and we had a straight-forward routine. I am now so glad that I have grown and matured in ways unthinkable, the joy and appreciation that my new life brings is indescribable. I am so thankful for growth and motivation; I now think as a wife that lives and breathes her family. After losing my mother in 2021 during our relocation to Arizona, I did not think my world could manage a blow so tough, but the fighter in me pushed hard and I know that it was the best decision my husband and I made. Her loss strengthened our bond and forced us to lean on to one another like never before. Our love is unshakable as well as our faith. I need him. So, this new chapter of my life, although it is a personal journey it is filled with spreading love and motivation to every single wife, woman, and mother I can reach. By the end of this book, you will familiarize yourself with strength, courage, and wisdom. You will become pregnant with peace and give birth to your passion. 10 years ago, I faced the fact that I needed to **get my sh*t together**, and today so will you. Everyone has a journey.

"When I dare to be powerful, to use my strength in the service of my vision, then it becomes less and less important whether I am afraid."

– Audre Lorde.

Laura's Journey

To know Laura is to love her, she is the first person called when someone is in need. She is one of the most selfless people I know, she is a great mother, wife, and friend. The only problem is that Laura just cannot seem to muster up the strength to pull herself up, she has become overwhelmed with ideas of what she would like to do with her life, but she just cannot seem to get out of her own way due to fear of failure. Laura attends seminars, webinars, and brunches, and invests a hefty amount of money investing in master-class courses but she has yet to start and use any of the valuable information she received. Laura can think of a million excuses as to why now is not a suitable time, she has become stuck whether she wants to admit it or not, Laura must change her mindset if she would like to reach her goals. Laura must get her ass up!

1

Get Your Sh*t and Get Up!

Feeling stuck, overwhelmed, and uninspired is completely normal. It is not a rare occurrence; it happened before in the past; it will happen again in the future. That is not where the danger is. What is detrimental is staying put, feeling like you are blocked, and unable to move. There is nothing you would love more than to take a step forward, yet you are so paralyzed by the fear of taking a step backward. So, what do you do? You stay put!

That is when you know you are in a stuck place. Not because you do not know where to go, what path to take, or how to advance, but because you are so anxious and overwhelmed that making the smallest decision can push you to the brink of a mental breakdown. You are excruciatingly aware of all the possibilities and ventures available to you, but you find the process of making up your mind painstaking, to say the least.

This analysis paralysis is what got you into the stuck place. You fluctuate between two complete opposites, a state of utter detachment, and a state of defeat. You do not care, then you care too much, you are unable to fulfill the most basic of tasks, then you work yourself to exhaustion, you do not socialize with others, you alienate your friends, then you overfill your schedule with meetings, appointments, and brunches.

You have slowly built a fortress around you, one that nobody can penetrate, yet you still expect others to know exactly what you are going through. The worst thing about feeling trapped and anxious is that you did not plan that trip to the stuck place. You suddenly find yourself a resident, but you have no idea how or why you got there. The one thing you are certain of is that you are not progressing, in fact, you are going nowhere.

It feels like everything around you is alive, vibrant, colorful, and loud, except you are at a halt, crushed by a deafening silence and a stifling darkness. You lock around you, trying to piece out where things went south, what wrong turns you took, how your life has gotten so out of hand when you have always taken pride in your ability to control everything down to the minute detail.

You stare at the suffocating stack of things you must do, things you must accomplish, goals you have set for yourself, long lost dreams that are evaporating into an eerie lull without meaning, without end. The buried sorrows of those unfulfilled promises you have made to yourself come to the surface, any glimmer of confidence you have had is fast eroding, and for the first time in forever, all you want to do is give up.

It seems almost pointless to get out of bed in the morning, the weight of the whole universe on your shoulders, the world crumbling right beneath your feet, taking any semblance of safety and security with it. You feel like a soulless corpse walking through impossibly narrow streets paved with forgotten ruins of haunted houses. You have become a mere shell of a person, you do not feel whole, so you try to fill up that gap with meaningless things, destructive habits, and toxic people.

You have gotten so much to do all the time that you feel defeated, unable to get started on even one small thing from what feels like a CVS receipt. So, nothing gets done, you dwell in your anxious thoughts, and wallow in self-pity, thinking that someone or something will eventually come and snatch you from the stuck place. Except, no one can save you but... *you*.

Recognizing you are stuck and acknowledging the fact that you need to make changes is the first step towards your journey of healing, forgiveness, and personal growth. You cannot conquer a monster if you do not know what it is and what it looks like.

Now that you know you are in the stuck place, you can start putting the pieces together to figure out the best way for you to get out of it, one that does not necessitate self-sacrifice or damaging compromises. You must trust the process, and yourself. Dealing with desperation has taught you that you are your greatest enemy. Overcoming these feelings will teach you that you are also your own hero, your greatest savior, and your dearest hope.

This book is aimed at giving you a fresh perspective on what has been setting you back your entire life. It is not just about conquering your fears, but most importantly, getting to the root of the problem, and why those worries, plague you in the first place. We are all susceptible to some degree of limiting beliefs. With that said, when those limiting beliefs start to not only affect your perception of the world, but your performance as well, that is when you need to take a step back, regroup, reevaluate, and work through those objections. It is time to get your shit and get up and this book will teach you just that!

Donna's Journey

Donna had a terrible childhood, being shifted to different foster homes due to her mother's addiction to drugs and neglect, unlike other children Donna never had her own bed, while transitioning to new homes everyone always "made a space" for her, as Donna grew older in the foster system, she continued to suffer abuse, this time sexual abuse by the father of the home. Donna wanted to tell, but for the first time in her life she had her own bed to lay in and she feared that if she were made to leave she would never have that again, so she kept quiet. Donna made a promise to herself that once an adult, no one would ever have this type of control over her again. Now an adult, Donna is a diligent worker and a great mother. She has her struggles, but the good outweighs the bad. The only problem is that Donna still allows her past to live rent-free inside of her head. She mentally relives her past trauma and longs for an apology, after all, Donna was a child then, and she never asked for any of this. One day Donna made the decision to seek therapy, you see the emotional trauma made it hard for Donna to love and accept love, she had never known what it was like to be loved properly so she would run, but Donna knew that something had to give. That trauma started to affect the way she would parent her children, the fear she had-had caused anxiety to let them be regular children, she has been trapped inside of her own thoughts of what if. As Donna continued in therapy, she found that she needed to forgive her abuser, now before you all say anything just keep reading about why forgiveness is so important, not to the perpetrator, but to the victim.

2

The Art of Forgiveness

*"It is one of the greatest gifts
you can give yourself, to forgive.
Forgive everybody."*

– Maya Angelou.

We often think that forgiveness is a luxury only a few can afford, that forgiveness will set you back and take your power away. This could not be further from the truth. You cannot move forward if you are still holding on to past hurts, regrets, and grudges. No matter what level of success you manage to achieve, your reluctance to forgive will always put you ten steps backward.

Your journey toward fulfillment and finding your purpose cannot advance if you are still living in memories of resentment and bitterness. Forgiveness is the greatest gift that you can give to yourself to rise above all the pain and suffering you have been subjected to. Forgiveness will propel you forward. It will free you from the relentless shackles of the past.

If you are curious about what it feels like to live the dream and lead a life that is fulfilling, meaningful, and values-based, you do not want to skip this chapter, as it provides deep insight into the path to take after you take back control.

Guilt is the most common obstacle you will encounter. You will feel guilty when you start putting yourself and your well-being first. So, you need to overcome that resistance and find support. Human beings do not come with a guide or manual. This means that everyone must learn the hard way that psychological processes can often end up being traps.

When you start to make progress, you soon realize that the harmful experiences you have been through did not necessarily have to unfold that way. In other situations where you have been the one to inflict harm, you start to look for a form of defense, something to justify the guilt, something like "my hands were tied," "I couldn't really do anything," etc.

Following that, you realize the harm that took place in the service of avoidance and maintaining a pre-made image of who you are. Relationships may have been broken needlessly, parents may have been put on blast too harshly, romantic partners may have been driven away unnecessarily, opportunities may have been lost pointlessly, and so on.

This is precisely when kindness and compassion are most needed. For you to accept these painful feelings, and defuse from harsh and critical thoughts, and focus on what you truly value, you must be kind to yourself. When you learn to do that, you take all that pain and suffering, and you make them part of your new, self-respectful, and values-consistent journey.

If your mind sends you an invitation to self-loathing and wallowing in guilt, respectfully decline. Do not beat yourself up for not reading the instructions manual you were never given. There is no need for defensive rationalizations of your past behavior. You did the best you could with the resources you had then. You know better now.

With that said, true growth requires more than just forgiving oneself, it is a process of forgiving others as well. It does not mean that what was done to you is justified or that you are letting that person off the hook for something incredibly damaging and traumatizing. It simply means that you are moving on, sliding off the hook yourself, beginning to serve your best interests, and prioritizing your sanity.

As this compassion deepens, you will start to see how avoidance and passivity have led you to destructive behavior towards yourself and others. Perhaps you were self-righteous or too self-absorbed. Or you were too distant, and you were not there for your loved ones.

These realizations are the other side of forgiveness, which is taking responsibility for your actions. When you identify patterns of destructive behavior, being responsible means cleaning up after your past self and the chaos it caused, so throughout your recovery, you are making repairs whenever and wherever you can.

Forgiveness does not entail forgetting about past wrongs, nor ignoring the pain you have suffered at the hand of a person or even yourself. It is not a sign of weakness, and it is not something you have to feel deep down before you move on to applying it to real-life situations.

Forgiveness is not condoning hurtful behavior either. It is a merciful and compassionate act that gives you back the control you did not or could not exhibit in the past. When you choose to forgive, you are also releasing that heavy burden you have been carrying your whole life, so you can finally begin to heal and move on.

You and you alone can do this. It is the best form of self-care you can show to yourself. This is how you get unstuck, how you stop being the victim, and how instead of sitting and waiting for a resolution that may never come, you are choosing to be an active performer and not a passive viewer.

Letting go will give you the freedom to move forward in your journey and to live the life of your dreams. Here is a four-step exercise to guide you through your forgiveness process.

> *Step #1: Awareness. Acknowledging the hurt and pain as it is without judgment.*

> *Step #2: Separation. Softening to encourage healing and repairs via your mindful self.*

> *Step #3: Compassion. Extending kindness to yourself and to others.*

> *Step #4: Letting go and moving on. Releasing resentment, anger, and grudges so you can finally direct your life toward the right path for you.*

The moment you decide to show kindness, compassion, and forgiveness to the world, you are not only affecting change within yourself, but you are also affecting change in everybody around you. When you release all of that stored negative energy, you also let go of the restraints that were holding you a prisoner of past injustices.

Now is the time to chart a new direction for yourself. From this point forward, you are relinquishing all the attachments and regrets of the past, but also the feelings of shame, guilt, anger, and pain. At this moment, you are in the drivers seat, you have control, and you decide how to move forward to get to the life you want to live.

Deon's Journey

Deon was the class clown; he was the funniest person in the whole school. Deon played sports, but just enough to get the girls attention. He was an only child, kind of spoiled. His father was there, but not in the capacity that Deon needed at the time. His mother worked tirelessly, but she always provided the things he wanted. What Deon needed was someone to lift him up, what we later found out was that Deon would be mad funny at school because he lacked attention at home. Deon's mom would be so upset about his behavior and lack of effort in school that she would verbally chew him out constantly. Deon's mother focused more on the negative things he did, but rarely acknowledged the positive. This would follow Deon into adulthood, he now felt as if he were not good enough at anything even life. Deon quit every job he had, fumbled opportunities given, allowed his anger and lack of confidence to affect his relationships and more. But one day Deon grew tired of holding on to his past and those that he felt contributed to his depression, he sat back and realized that he was in a place where only he could decide how his story would end, not those nay-sayers. Deon joined a local gym, cleared his mind, gained a trade, and found his passion, on that day Deon decided to use his past as fuel to boost him into his purpose. Deon chose life.

3

Break Through

> *"If you feel lost, disappointed,*
> *hesitant, or weak, return to yourself,*
> *to who you are, here and now and when you*
> *get there, you will discover yourself, like a*
> *lotus flower in full bloom, even in a muddy*
> *pond, beautiful and strong."*
>
> – Masaru Emoto.

You continue making the same mistakes. The past should be useful. From the past, we learn what works and what does not, provided the experience is interpreted correctly. Do you ignore your past? Well, it is easy to do but it has negative consequences. Do you realize that time does not heal all wounds? Healing heals all wounds. If there is something in your past you feel the desire to forget, it is hurting you in the present. In many cases you have adopted negative attitudes, beliefs, or behavioral characteristics from your parents. Do you have the same short temper your father had? Do you lie excessively like your mother did? Do you mistrust rich people? Dislike anyone that is a democrat? Beliefs and attitudes that you did not choose for yourself can be damaging to your self-image. Did you know that a single negative experience is affecting your belief system today? These experiences are most likely to occur in childhood but are not limited to your early years.

THERE ARE SIGNS THAT YOU'RE NOT USING YOUR PAST CONSTRUCTIVELY: Here is an example:

You did not do well in art class in Fourth grade.

You may have drawn the conclusion that:

- You have no artistic ability.

- Your art teacher did not like you.

- Your art teacher was not a good teacher.

- You are not a good person because you are not good at creating art.

- You lack any creative ability.

- You are not good at learning new skills.

- You are not very smart.

- You are not a well-rounded person.

And it can snowball from there. Suppose one of your classmates made fun of your drawing in art class.

- I am not a good enough.

- People do not like me.

- I should not let anyone see something as personal as my artwork in the future.

I will avoid exposing myself to any criticism in the future by being very reserved and cautious.

Now do you see how negative and erroneous beliefs can develop from negative experiences?

These beliefs can be extremely limiting and influence every part of your life.

So now I need you to question the belief. Most of your beliefs are not justified if you examine them closely. This is a key step.

- Where did this belief come from? Is the source credible?

Is it based on sufficient evidence? One experience usually is not enough. Touching a hot stove is sufficient experience to draw a valid conclusion. One failed attempt at dating or starting a business is not.

- Is the belief reasonable?

Determine what the belief is costing you. Inaccurate beliefs can cause damage. What are the beliefs you hold about yourself costing you?

- A lack of confidence.

- Lower-income.

- Fewer friends or a dissatisfying social life.

- The belief that your options are limited to change your life.

- Overall dissatisfaction with yourself or your life.

I personally think that you should choose an alternate belief that better suits reality and supports a healthy self-image. Convince yourself that your new belief is possible. Always remember that your past does not define you, it should be used as fuel to get you where you are destined to go.

Deborah's Journey

Deborah was an exceptional woman; she was a provider and an advocate for her children and others. She was a diligent worker, been a well-respected employee on her job for over 44 years. Deborah never met a stranger. As a grandmother, Deborah would do everything in her power just to see the excitement in her grandchildren's eyes. Deborah was a straight shooter; she spoke plainly and what you saw was what you got. She lived unapologetically, she helped those in need, she fed anyone that she believed was hungry, she provided shelter and love to people. But the most amazing thing Deborah did in her 66 years on earth was that she lived everyday finding joy in each moment, Deborah is no longer with us today, she passed June 7, 2021. Deborah is my mother, and one thing she always taught us was "'Weeping may endure for a night, but joy comes in the morning" so keep pushing and keep smiling, your best days are just ahead.

4

Find the Joy

> *"When a defining moment*
> *comes along, you can do one*
> *of two things. Define the moment*
> *or let the moment define you."*
>
> – Roy McAvoy.

If you find yourself often either pondering on how life used to be or anxious about the future, then you are going to live either a sad or anxious life. The past is gone, and the future is yet to happen. But the present is where we are now. It is where we can prepare for the future and make friends with the past. We can learn from the past and prepare for the future. However, if we stay hung up on one or the other, then our lives will unfold without us realizing what we are sacrificing in the process of dwelling on what could have been or what can be. It is important to understand that "living in the moment" is not an excuse to forget about your past or ignore what the future holds, it is simply a way that we can be more mindful of our time. Living in the present has a lot of benefits that will bless our life with more prosperity and happiness, here are a few:

Dwelling in nostalgia is letting the past control our future:

The past should be used to understand ourselves and learn from our mistakes. The past is a memory and a recollection of events that have already happened and will not happen again. It is important to keep the past in perspective, but we should not let the past dictate our future by being hung up on it. We develop, we evolve, and we get better. Our ideas become better, our bodies change, and our perspectives may even mature.

Living in the now is realizing the power we have:

We have the power to change our future if we try. However, changing the future happens neither in the past nor the future, it happens now. Every second that has gone by is a second you can never get back, and every minute in the future is not guaranteed. While we have so much power to change the future, we have no guarantee of living the next minute.

You will stop waiting:

Getting trapped in either the past or the future can leave you almost paralyzed and unsure of what to do. Therefore, people will often fear taking a big leap and just 'wait for tomorrow.' People will often waste their days being anxious about a tomorrow that has not happened yet or a yesterday that will never happen again.

You will enjoy life more:

By understanding the power of now and why it is so important to live in the moment, you will be a lot more careful when it comes to how you choose to spend your time. By realizing that tomorrow is not guaranteed, you will not waste another second and live life to the fullest as if today is your last day.

You become more mindful:

Being grateful for each moment you live is important for enjoying the present. It helps you stop reminiscing on 'the good old days' and puts you in the driver's seat when it comes to creating the life you want to live rather than the life you once lived or the life you could live.

You will improve your relationships:

We are often looking for the next moment always reaching forward for the future which can hurt our relationships. Relationships are about the journey and not the end goal. Therefore, despite being so close to your significant other, you might seem extremely far away in your thoughts and worries. By living in the moment, you will savor every little detail of the present and truly value your relationships.

How to Live in the Moment

- **Cherish the Journey:** The journey to climbing the mountain and seeing the world at the top is far sweeter than the sight (end goal).

- **Be More Mindful of Your Time:** realize that time is your most valuable asset. While you might lose a million dollars and make it back, you can never get back a single minute of your life.

- **Pay Attention to the Intricate Details:** notice the world around you and be thankful for the experiences you have.

- **Meditate Often:** One of the best ways to elevate your energy and be more in control of your mind is to practice meditating. It can help you make sense of the world around you as well as how you view the world.

Cathy's Journey

Imagine your life moving forward, you have so many ideas, so many opportunities to become the person you have always wanted to be. Now imagine your lack of motivation to get these things done. Cathy has so many things going for herself, so many people in her corner pushing her forward, but Cathy just cannot seem to find the motivation that she needs to start, five kids, single, educated but the constant fight each day has Cathy feeling hopeless. Cathy now needs to find her reason and dig in, one thing about life it will continue no matter what. Cathy has now started working harder to find herself, she is taking the necessary steps to become bolder, improved. Cathy is now realizing that she cannot wait on others to motivate her, but that it must be inside of her to achieve the goal she set for herself. Cathy will need to drown out the outside noise and keep her eye on the prize. Oftentimes distractions can come in the form of people, social media, social groups, toxic relationships, and lack of confidence. Find your purpose because you have shit to do.

5

Find Your Reason

> *"He who has a "why" to live*
> *can bear almost any how."*
>
> – Friedrich Nietzsche.

Not everyone is going to have pleasant things to say to or about you all the time, especially once you set goals and start working towards them. After all, many people do not have the strength to do so, and misery loves company. You must find your reason – your reasons for trying to succeed – and those motives need to be strong enough to get you through even the hardest of times.

Finding your reason is easy if you are honest with yourself and willing to take chances with your time, energy, and thought processes. What happens to you happens for a reason, so why not let that reason be to make you a more successful person? What does not kill you only makes you stronger.

If all else fails, the love of the fight for success could be your reason for holding on. In the meantime, you will find that you end up surprised by how far you can go past the point where you thought it was the end. If you determine your reasons for wanting to succeed in the first place, and you remind yourself of those reasons often, you will find it much easier to muster the courage it takes to keep going in the face of great adversity.

Your personal reason should be something that cannot be shaken or swayed by anything. It should be something that gets you going and encourages you, especially when you fail. Your reasons for wanting to succeed must outlast the test of time and persistence, and it must mean something special to you.

How we approach the inevitabilities of life is what determines our fate. Being afraid to fail, not knowing where to start, allowing yourself to become discouraged, seeing only the negative in any given situation – these are all ways never to be successful. If you want to get the most out of your efforts, you are going to have to find ways to get inspired and motivated to do so. Someone's opinion of you or the outcome of any given situation never has to become your reality.

Getting inspired and motivated to do anything is simple if you follow these three simple steps:

- *Step One: Define what you want without paying attention to unreasonable limits.*

- *Step Two: Think about how the world will be if you do not act.*

- *Step Three: Have someone hold you accountable for your claims and promises.*

Remember that your obstacles are only as significant as you allow them to be. If there is a will then there is a way. Stepping out of your comfort zone and becoming more willing to do things that you do not necessarily like will get you far on the path to success. No matter what you do or how you get there, be sure you keep your eyes focused on the road.

Stay Focused on the Road

If you allow yourself to gain inspiration and motivation from the events of the world around you, you will be able to channel those emotions into everything you do. Act with apprehension and fear, however, and you may find yourself becoming lost in a sea of choices. Remember that you must stand for something or else you will fall for anything.

No matter what you must do, make sure that you always stay focused on your goal. If you always keep your objective in the back of your mind, instead of repeating those nasty and negative thoughts to yourself, all your actions will line up to have your back. Eventually, you will begin to see progress. It is as simple as that.

The way in which you focus your mind plays a huge role in how successful you end up being. If you see nothing but obstacles, you will become discouraged and feel comfortable giving up. However, if you look at those obstacles as opportunities to be effective, then you will find it easier to keep going with a focused point of view.

If possible, select an accountability partner from your friends, family, or coworkers. This person should be someone who can be trusted and who can help you stay on track. On top of that, your accountability partner should make sure you are achieving your goals and sticking to any promises you make. This person should also be good at helping you prioritize so that you do not make any promises you cannot keep.

Finding an accountability partner is not easy, thus we must make the journey to success on our own. That does not mean that success is impossible. The fact that you are a loner on the road to success is just one more obstacle to overcome. When you finally do, you will be able to look back at the positive difference you made all by yourself.

Know Your Goals

Having dreams and ambitious is one extraordinarily strong driving force in life. Having dreams that you want to achieve keeps you going. I know I want to achieve financial freedom and that is the reason I keep working. I want to be this in 2 years' time, I want to be a successful writer at the end of the year, by 2025, I want to be a PhD holder. These dreams and aspirations keep people going in life. You know what you want to do with your life and what you want to achieve in days or months and that makes you focused, it keeps you going regardless of how hard it might be now. When determining your goals, do not just try to focus on something that might be unattainable. As a high school student, your goal cannot be to be richer than Jeff Bezos at the end of the semester. You should dream big, but you should also be realistic. When you set unrealistic goals, you might find yourself nowhere close to your ambitions in the set time and that might only frustrate your efforts.

Maintain a Positive Mindset:

Regardless of what hurdles you might encounter, remain positive. Even when it feels like nothing is working for you now, remain positive. Positivity helps you get through life. When little life challenges come knocking at your door, the best approach to this is to just remain positive. Life cannot always be bad, it will not always be good either, so having a negative mindset will not help you in the way. Simply breaking a mug in the morning and you have already considered that as a sign that you will have a difficult day will end up with you having that difficult day, so why not just be positive instead, it will not hurt you in any way.

Find it Now:

We already discussed finding your reason, but after that, you also need to find your purpose. You need to know why you want this. You need to know why you might want to give up. Why do you want to give up on your dream? Why do you feel like you should quit? Why do you want to change your dreams? You need to ask yourself why and be very honest with yourself when answering these questions. When you find value in what you are doing, you will understand why exactly you need to keep going and keep pushing.

Be Intentional:

Motivation does not just happen; you must be intentional about it. Have goals and set a schedule or structure to those goals. You must be intentional about achieving these goals. Most of us have new year resolutions every year that we never even pay attention to, writing a new list every year, knowing fully well that we are writing it just because. However, when we are setting our goals and dreams, the driving force in the direction of our lives and future, we need to be very intentional about it. You do not decide on your future goals out of boredom, or just for the fun of it, it not a joke, this is your life. Be serious about your goals and be intentional towards its attainment.

Celebrate Your Wins:

Whether small or big achievements, you achieved something and that is worth celebrating. Encourage yourself when you achieve set goals, celebrate it because even the small wins matter. When you achieve set objectives, celebrate them, and set new objectives for yourself. That motivates you to continue achieving your goals.

Judy's Journey

Judy was a single parent as the result of an unplanned pregnancy, the relationship with the father was non-existent. The two decided that it was best to co-parent the child, but it was made mutually clear that there would be no chance at a family. Judy appeared to understand, but as time would pass Judy became enraged at the fact that her life had now become exactly what she despised most. The reality that she had now become a "baby momma" hurt her to her core. Judy tried hard to hold her head and co-parent, but life found a way to always threw her short comings in her face. She would now have to watch the child's father move forward with his life, he would go on to have more children and seek new relationships. Although Judy's communication with him was solely about their son, she could not help wondering why she had not found a "love" of her own and how could he just go on with his life so easily. Granted Judy was not interested in being with her son's father, but she wondered why wasn't she good enough for him to at least try? These questions rattled Judy's brain constantly, especially when asked by family and friends. One day at their scheduled drop off, Judy decided to just ask out of respectful curiosity "Why did we never try? What was it about me, that made you decide to not push for a family with our son? What the father said next had Judy floored, "It was not you Judy, I slept with a woman whom I did not know and that was not the plan I had for my life, I knew I needed to take responsibility for our child, but there was no way that I could force myself to fall in love just because of that. It would not be fair to myself, you, or our child." At that moment Judy realized that she was not the only one that had a plan for their life, she told him "Thank you for this and thank you for protecting our child." As if a weight had been lifted from her shoulders, Judy was relieved. All this time she believed that she was the problem, oftentimes we give ourselves too much credit, other people have goals set also. Now after understanding this, Judy needed to learn to forgive herself, Judy had been holding on to the anger of being a "single woman" so much that it caused animosity and bitterness, so in return any man that approached her had to hear of it, while learning that it was a huge red flag for men, Judy decided to set her pride aside and seek happiness, she began to smile more, she starting working on herself so much that her confidence began to rise and men from everywhere noticed her new glow. Judy chose life, oftentimes we demand our lives to go in a different direction, but God is the director, and all is forgiven. Judy decided that she was not her circumstances and worthy of love. Judy is married to a wonderful man, and they have a beautiful family.

6

Pride Aside

The problem with pride is that it is a constant tug of war between pride itself and self-esteem. While you need to have respect for yourself, it can be a slippery slope toward the destructiveness of pride. There are reasons people struggle with pride, and it is not that hard to figure out why. Self-actualization is one of the last stages in Maslow's hierarchy of needs. To achieve this level, you need to have the other needs covered already. However, the problem comes in esteem. It is quite easy to confuse esteem with pride. In fact, people think of them as synonymous. If you are sincere when it comes to getting it together, you must get this straight.

Pride is harmful, self-esteem is rewarding, and getting to the level where you let go of pride can be one of the most liberating and freeing moments in your life.

Which is it? Pride or confidence?

One of the biggest problems with pride is that it is so close to confidence. Being confident in yourself is especially important but being overly confident is just as bad as having no confidence. It is important to realize that confidence is a belief in the fact that you are able to meet life's challenges successfully. However, it is far from the notion that a person is better than anyone and better than themselves.

Why pride will poison your life:

One of the most obvious downfalls of pride is that it makes you blind to improvement. If you are overly confident and have pride, you think you do not need to improve and get better as a person because of course, you are the best. If you are full of pride, you will also tend to overlook areas of growth. Everyone has flaws, but it takes a confident and humble individual to call them areas where they can improve.

Social Repellant:

If you have ever read Dale Carnegie's *How to Win Friends and Influence People,* you will realize that the best way to win over people's hearts is to listen to them. People love talking about themselves including their opinion, their loved ones, their favorite sports team, what they think is the best food, and their emotions. If you care about making an impact on people whether it be people outside of your social circle or people close to you, then you must hear what people have to say. Pride makes you think that this is the silliest thing in the world. People's emotions and concerns are trivial to you, and they are mere dribble. This will make you very unlikable to people and you will gently pull people away from you.

Having pride makes you think that what you are doing is the right thing. First, it will disguise itself as confidence, then it will convince you that you just protecting yourself from other people who can take advantage of you or waste your time. It will not be long before you will be convinced that pride is good, and it will not seem like pride. Once you lose your social circle and you have no one that cares for you, pride will make you think that this is a good thing because all those people that have been chased out of your life wanted to take advantage of you anyway and if they really liked you then they would have never abandoned you. That is how easy it is to fall into the jaws of pride.

Being Vulnerable Makes You Strong, Pride Makes You Weak:

If you are infected with pride, I am sure that you will cringe when you hear: "Being Vulnerable makes you strong, pride makes you weak." Being vulnerable is not what you think, it is not letting people walk all over you or have people harass you. Vulnerability is accepting your flaws, insecurities, and weaknesses. Think about it, if you know every single insecurity you have, how can you be harmed? By knowing how weak you are, doesn't that make you strong? It is certainly a tough choice to let go of pride and show your humanity in humility.

There is a subtle yet major change that happens in your personality once you accept your weaknesses, it is very minuscule, but there is a moment when the magic happens. Once you combine confidence in your ability to overcome challenges and the awareness that you are weak and vulnerable in other areas, you will be totally freed and inch closer to self-actualization.

Becoming Free of Pride:

This change in behavior is not going to come overnight, it requires diligent work and consistent mindset training. Here are steps and guidelines to help you with that:

Be More of a Spectator:

If you are ever at a social event with a few people, practice listening more and seeing what others do very intently. Do not confuse this with holding back your emotions or what you want to say. Instead, truly become a spectator and listen to what people, their reactions, who do they look at the most, who speaks first and last, and how they change when you talk about something they like.

Family First:

People of faith believe that family union with God is what helps people have a better cause and motivation. In short, when two people get married and have offspring, they do not work hard for themselves, instead, they work hard for their children and significant other. There is a magnificent shift of energy when you go from being on your own to having a reason to work hard. Therefore, putting your family first before anything and even before yourself can help you achieve a stoic mindset free of pride.

Be Willing to Apologize:

Having the strength to admit that you are wrong to yourself and to others is important in the fight against pride. It is not just about the act of apologizing to other people, but it is accepting their reaction after apologizing whatever it may be.

Let Go of Defensiveness:

One of the most common ways you can see pride rotting away at people is when they get defensive when they are confronted with a fact. The accuracy of the confrontation is irrelevant, what is important is that there is a reaction of defensiveness. Being defensive makes you hard to communicate with and it is a clear sign of weakness. The inability to deal with a complaint, a confrontation, or a demanding situation before wanting to save face is very obviously weak and a sign of pride.

Practice Humility

"Humility must accompany all our actions, must be with us everywhere, for as soon as we glory in our good works they are of no further value to our advancement in virtue."

– Saint Augustine.

By letting go of pride, you need to practice humility, it is a virtue that will help you in many aspects of life. When you are humble, you tend to focus more on yourself. You become a better listener and thinker which helps you in your personal development and growth. Pride will not let you see things clearly the way they are. When you find someone better than you, you start to develop hatred and when you cannot beat that person, you start looking for flaws in that person to make yourself feel better. Humility on the other hand will help you accept that you cannot always be better than everybody and when you see people who are better than you, you study them and learn from them, using them to improve yourself and your skills in the best way possible.

Carmen's Journey

Her friend's spend time together constantly, at the bar buying drinks, maxing out credit cards and living well above their means. Carmen used to spend so much time and money trying to keep up until one day she sat back and realized that she could not afford to, unlike her friends Carmen has a goal she has been reaching for, she promised herself that by the age of 30 she will become a homeowner, the first in her family. Carmen has expressed this dream of hers to her friends but because their goal differs from hers, they do not see what the big deal is to spend and live carelessly. Carmen struggles to save and even though she is close to her goal, she notices that she is left spending the most after each outing, it's her car being used for every trip, her hot spot, her apartment and more. It has become exhausting, and the friendship is obviously one sided. Carmen finally realizes that her "friends" simply have nothing to lose and that she must step back no matter how they feel, Carmen decided to put herself first.

7

Nothing to Lose

> *"Don't engage with someone*
> *with nothing to lose.*
> *It is an unequal fight."*
>
> – Baltasar Gracián.

There is power in having nothing to lose. The top ultra-wealthy in the world have had no inheritance and they did not come from a family that gave them the opportunity to be great in life. In other words, they are people who had nothing to lose. It is particularly important to familiarize yourself with this notion as it can help you understand the behaviors you see around you. There is a debate around which is more dangerous, a person who has everything to lose or a person who has nothing. Regardless of who is more dangerous and who has the edge, the person who has nothing to lose can be dangerous and they have a different mindset.

The mindset of having nothing to lose is so powerful that it was introduced in the Army for people with high-risk missions. Taking a young man with no girlfriend, wife, children, faith, home, or prospects for a career is one of the criteria for these soldiers, but there is training that can enhance the mentality of war. Think about it, if someone has nothing to lose and everything to gain, they will try everything under the sun because they cannot lose. In fact, they might even destroy themselves in the process because they just truly do not care.

Once you have nothing and you recognize that you do in fact have nothing, a great weight will be lifted off your shoulders and you will feel a different type of courage. However, courage in the sense that you have nothing to lose and anything you do is good even if it ends up in failure. This relentless mindset is truly vicious and powerful. While it has helped people take enormous decisions that changed their lives, it can be self-destructive. For instance, most immigrants from poor third-world countries are from the ones that experience destitution the most. In fact, most people in those countries want to immigrate to a better country that can guarantee their freedom, well-being, and financial situation, but the ones that go are extremely impoverished because they truly have nothing to lose. This is exactly the type of mentality that makes people travel by foot in the scolding desert or the ruthless winters for weeks just to get to a better place.

The Ones that Have Nothing to Lose:

You obviously cannot completely avoid people who have nothing to lose but you need to know and study them. People who have nothing to lose will not care about people who do have something to lose. If you have a job, a loved one, parents, money, an apartment, things you enjoy doing, then you have something to lose. However, instead of thinking of it as a weakness, let it fuel your motivation to overcome challenges in life.

Beware when it comes to the type of people who are close to you and have nothing to lose. These are the type of people that enjoy the nothingness they are in because it fuels their motivation. By not having anything to lose, they can overcome fears which people who have something to lose are worried about.

Having Nothing to Lose or
Having Everything to Lose:

People in positions of power recognize the power of not having anything to lose because they were once that person. The hunger for more and lack of fear is a surefire way to overcome any concern you once had. However, the person who has everything to lose is just as powerful because they recognize the value of the things they might lose. If you have a family that you love, you know exactly what I am talking about.

On the one hand, someone with nothing to lose will go to great extremes to take what they want. They might resort to tactics that the person with everything will not go to because they are risky. However, considerable risk is often associated with high reward. On the other hand, a person who has everything to lose is not short of motivation to keep fighting. An example of this is living with a family, if you live by yourself and there is some type of danger, you will not care as much as you would if you had small children and a spouse. Fighting for a cause is a whole lot easier when you have a cause that is other than yourself.

Relationships

In romantic relationships, it is important to ensure that the other person has a cause. If the other person has nothing to lose, why would they care for you? Most people with this mindset can never genuinely love another person because loving someone entails that you want the best for them which is often being with them. If someone is in love with someone else, then they have something to lose.

Friends

A bad company usually consists of people who have no appreciation for what is good in life, and they will not care about what you can lose. Good friends will not let you be self-destructive because they know what you can lose. They will not let you destroy yourself because they want the best for you, and they know the things you can lose.

.

Work

People with nothing to lose are very destructive when it comes to the workplace. They fail to appreciate the good things in life that they already have and will be dangerous to themselves and to others.

Jolene's Journey

Jolene's hustles each day to get her kids ready for school and daycare, she packs lunch, she kisses them and off they go. Jolene is often the first inside of the office each day, preparing the coffee, checking emails, preparing for meetings, and taking a mental note of what to grab from the grocery store on the way home. Jolene, a single middle-aged mother of three seems to never complain, she just gets it done. Jolene's ex-husband of 13 years made the choice to leave his family and marry his assistant who is 20 years younger, but that is another story that will require therapy and wine. As Jolene puts on her "big girl" spanx each day, it reminds her of the trivial things that it takes to make her world work. While family and friends think that she is insane she manages it all, Jolene simply gives thanks each day. Thankful for the ability to press forward, thankful that she never allowed the enemy to win, thankful that her children are all well, thankful that she has surrounded herself with support. Jolene also lost a total of fifty-eight pounds after finalizing her divorce and she could not feel any better especially after seeing the look on her ex-husband's face at their son's football game, you would have thought he seen a ghost. Jolene learned to be thankful even amid a storm.

8

Gratitude

> *"Learn to rise up and be thankful, for if we didn't learn a lot today, at least we learnt a little and if we didn't learn a little, at least we didn't get sick and if we got sick, at least we didn't die; so, let us be thankful."*
>
> – Buddha.

A big part of losing your pride and being more open to the world of possibilities is quite simple yet extremely challenging for many. Saying thank you can be one of the most rewarding and it will give you a sense of belonging. While you might think of the words "thank you" as trivial and transparent in the world of everyday expressions, its meaning goes beyond a formality. On the surface, saying thank you is a formality and a social lubricant, but thank you holds a deeper meaning that is related to gratitude.

Gratitude may be one of the most overused terms for self-improvement, but it is not based on shaky grounds. In fact, research has shown that being thankful and grateful can help you and others achieve a higher level of happiness and self-fulfillment. Research has shown that gratitude can help you be more positive which in turn can decrease stress. The study took a group that wrote blessings about things in their lives, they had to write on the good things that happened in their life and be grateful for them. The other group was told to write about their irritations during the day. The group that wrote positive things about their day felt more optimistic, had better health, and had fewer visits to physicians. They were also more initiative-taking when it comes to changing things around and exercised more often.

Other studies also show the importance of showing gratitude in relationships. Couples who express their gratitude had better communication thus overcoming some of the challenges that come with relationships. The same goes for the workplace as another study found that managers who said the word "thank you" more often had better results since employees work harder and have been more satisfied with their job.

Saying thank you must be the easiest and simplest way to express gratitude. Saying thank you to your loved one, your coworkers, your life, parents, and everyone that you interact way is an effortless way to bring joy into your life and it takes no effort.

People want to feel appreciated for their efforts and this is a fact that you must accept from now on. If you have ever worked in a managerial position, you know how important it is to be show gratitude and express how proud you are of them. As a result, this will make them happy and who does not want to make people happy.

Exchanging Positive Energy:

One of the biggest misconceptions is that saying thank you gives people power and takes power away from you. First, this is a terrine way of thinking about social dynamics, no one is keeping score on who has the most power and there is no reward to the "toughest." In fact, saying thank you can make you the leader in many ways. Gratitude can help you be more grateful, but it also makes others appreciate you more. This exchange of positive energy can light up any social circumstance and make your relationships more fluid.

How to Cultivate Gratitude:

Gratitude is something you cultivate; it is something you develop and maintain. Therefore, you need to practice gratitude more often with people around you and with yourself.

Keep a Gratitude Journal:

It might seem overwhelming to write in a journal but remember that beginnings are always going to be slow. Make it a habit to keep a gratitude section in your journaling book every day. This is not for others to see; this is merely a record of your gratitude to others around you and to the world itself. Journaling is an activity that is beneficial to you.

When you are feeling stress or tensioned, you can easily pick up your journal and write down your feelings, you feel better by just writing them down. It is just like therapy, how you feel better by talking to someone but in this instance, it is just you, your journal, and your emotions. Writing something you are thankful for every time has the power to keep you in a good mood and keep you motivated. It becomes a habit to fill up your gratitude section every time. After wringing about other things that might have been stressful during the day, you find yourself eager to write in your gratitude section because you know it will lift your mood.

Write a Thank-You Note:

You can easily make someone's day by just sending them light but impactful thank you note. This note can discuss how you are so happy with someone's presence in your life, how they have impacted you, how you made better choices thanks to them, and that you believe in them. It does not have to be regular as it needs to be sincere and honest.

Pray:

Any religious person can tell you how they have changed the way they thought about praying once they got older. When you are young, prayer seems like a chore, but the older you get, the more you realize that prayer can bring peace and serenity into your life. It also helps your gratitude to God.

Appreciate Positivity:

Gone are the days that you must ruin your day because of someone's energy. You must not ever deal with someone's negativity anymore because I am sure that you have had it. As much as you hate negativity, it is important to be appreciative of the positive energy around you. This can be the people you love such as your family and friends or even those that you have crossed paths with, and they made a tremendous change in your life for the better.

Appreciate the Moment

Learn to appreciate every passing moment and be positive through it all. Appreciate the pure white snowflakes, Appreciate the beauty of the sunset, appreciate the morning sun that guides you to a new day, appreciate the coworker that thought of you and got you coffee, appreciate the distant friend who reached out to you for the first time in years to check how you are doing, the friend who will always come to keep you company because you are an introvert with no social life whatsoever. When you learn to appreciate these basic things that you experience in your daily life, it will help you cultivate the habit of gratitude. You will be able to appreciate every little thing anyone does for you or that happened to you.

Acts of Service

Do something nice today. Act kindly and do something to people around you, it might not be much but its fine if it brings a smile to their face. When people around you are happy, all of you will be smiling more and become happier. You can just think about something that someone around you will appreciate and will not be detrimental to you and help them with it. By doing this, you focus on people around you and see the type of smiles your little act of service has brought to your face and it encourages you to do better, it also makes you more appreciative of the little things people do for you because you realize what it takes do those little things for people.

Daily Gratitude

Which people in my life have taught

me about unconditional love?

____

____

____

What are some of your personality traits

for which you are most thankful?

____

____

____

What family members am I most grateful

for? What makes them so special?

____

____

____

What is something nice that another

person did for me this week?

____

____

____

What is something nice that I did for

another person this week?

____

____

____

What is something that I recently noticed that

made me realize how fortunate I am?

____

____

____

What are three things I could do today to be a

kinder and more compassionate person?

____

____

____

What do I really appreciate about my life?

____

____

____

What are five things that happened to me that strengthened

my character and made me who I am today?

____

____

____

How can I continue being more thankful?

____

____

____

Paris's Journey

He cheated. He broke my heart in every imaginable way. He spent so much time grooming me to become weak and vulnerable, I never saw it coming, I never thought in a million years that he would leave me with nothing. I felt that because I was his wife, that the title alone carried weight and a bond that no one could break. 2 years in, I found out that I was pregnant, everyone around me was ecstatic, I was devastated, devastated because I knew that I was stuck with this shell of a man that used his power to control my life. He knew that he could bullshit his way both in and out of the hearts of people, which made them feel as if I were lying when I would try to get away. He never hit me, he would just hit around me, break things, punch things and then tell me that I was next. After the birth of our daughter, I looked into her beautiful hazel eyes, and I planned our escape. I never thought I would have the courage to leave, although I knew was not coming a part of me wondered if God would just tear him apart, make him hurt, make him lose everything, take him to his lowest place so I could laugh in his face just as he did me. Please God I begged, but God assured me that the blessing that was just ahead for me, would require me to never look back nor speak ill of that man again, He showed me that if I just focus on what I need, He will take care of the rest. I, Paris learned the art of healing privately.

9

Hurt Publicly, Heal Privately

> *"Just like there is time for pain,*
> *there is always time for healing."*
>
> – Jennifer Brown.

So, you have been dealt a bad hand lately got hurt publicly. Getting hurt is a very normal and mundane thing that can happen to anyone. But it certainly leaves its mark on our psyche. If you have had an encounter where you were tested in front of other people, you know how much it stings. Here in this chapter, we are going to discuss this issue and how to deal with it.

What Not to Do:

Being hurt is not easy and it might be a natural reflex to lash out or do things that have no benefit to you. It is important to realize that this situation is as bad as it is, so make sure that you minimize the damage. Here are things you should not do if you are hurt publicly.

Lash Out:

This is the immediate reaction that ninety-nine percent of people have when it comes to getting hurt. Someone made you feel bad, so you just want to make them feel as well, give' em a taste of their own medicine. However, this is a terrible idea as it displays how much of an impact that moment had on you.

Being Defensive:

Do not try to be defensive and try to save face in a situation like this. It is important that you understand how your brain works in a situation when you are hurt emotionally in front of people. The wrong approach is to try to fix the situation by making yourself look a bit better, but it just makes you look worse.

Turning the Tables Around:

Another immediate reaction people have is trying to hurt the other person as well. Say you were confronted with a substandard performance at work by a manager and then another employee adds fuel to the fire. Avoid coming back at them by mentioning bad qualities they have as this just makes you seem spiteful and childish.

How You Can Turn This Around:

If you have never been hurt publicly, you eventually will experience this, and it will sting. Now that we have dealt with things you should not do, let us talk about what you should do.

Do Not Kill the Messenger:

Let us be reasonable at first and have a good heart. If someone has something to say, let us hear it first. We tend to hate the messenger more than we hate the message itself. This is quite common since most "messages" come from people we do not like such as bosses or managers. First, you should hear the message and listen to what they have to say. However, you must be very attentive and use reason with not a single ounce of emotion. If they are trying to hurt you for the sake of it to make you feel bad, do not take it seriously and just see it as a sad turn of events because they are also hurt. If someone is so toxic that they want to make others feel bad, God knows what they are dealing with. So just bless their soul and move on. However, if they are saying something that you are insecure about and they are right, then you must address it. Say for instance that you have indeed been slacking at work, well then you have been, and it has nothing to do with emotions. This is your battle to fight.

Acknowledge their Message:

Do you want to know the best way to diffuse a situation? Just acknowledge someone's' feelings. If someone has something to say to you, say "I understand how you feel, and thank you for bringing that up." This is likely to stop them right at their tracks with no more hateful things to say.

Heal Privately:

The most important part of this discussion is healing. Now if you have been hurt because the other person just wants you to be hurt, then just understanding that they are troubled and corrupt at heart will make those hurt feelings dissipate. However, if the person is right on what they have been saying, then you need to address this.

Do What You Can:

You need to make sure that you do what you can to ensure that you are doing better. We must seek better ways to get better in life whether it be for our work, relationships, health, or spirituality. If you have been hurt, then the best way to deal with it is to privately heal.

Do it for You:

Do not do this for other people to see that you are healing. Posting online about how you are healing and getting better just makes you look like you are not healed at all. If you have been hurt in a relationship, then heal on your own without involving anyone else. This is your own battle to fight and while you might lose a fight, you are not going to lose the war.

Healing From What Hurts

What secrets am I holding onto that are causing me harm?

____

____

____

Am I willing to uncover the root of

my pain? Why or why not?

____

____

____

Do I examine the mistakes I made from

a place of judgment or kindness?

____

____

____

What do I need to forgive my younger self

for not understanding or realizing?

What anger or frustration am I

struggling to let go of and why?

What are five things that my best self would

do that I am currently not doing?

What have I been putting off that

can help me heal and why?

____

____

____

Chloe's Story

Chloe is a beautiful woman, single, well educated, well-traveled and extremely popular amongst her friends. Chloe has always been the kind of woman that danced to the beat of her own drum, she never needed a crowd however everyone would always "cling" to her. Graduated top of her class from a prestigious university and through challenging work and determination she was fortunate enough to snag her dream job. Everything in Chloe's life is top tier except for her choice in men, you see Chloe comes from a two-parent home that most would die for, but no one knew that Chloe's mother was being abused verbally each day by her father, she was belittled and made to feel inadequate throughout her marriage to Chloe's father. As a child Chloe would hear the harsh words and slowly, she started to wear the words she heard. Chloe has fought so hard to become who she is all to allow the wrong shit to come in a shape her future. At some point Chloe must become strong enough to understand that her past does not dictate her future. She is not the words she heard, that in fact she is enough woman for anyone that has been blessed to be in her presence, but she must believe within.

10

You Allowed It

Boundaries are an essential part of producing and reflecting a healthy self-image. When a person has strong healthy boundaries, they implicitly communicate confidence and self-respect to the world. Further, this goes to show that they are aware of their worth and they can clearly demonstrate their value.

Healthy boundaries not only make us feel good about ourselves but also protect our personal integrity. If you do not set and maintain healthy boundaries, you are practically telling others that you are at their mercy.

So, in a way you allow them to dictate your thoughts, feelings, emotions, and behavior. In addition to that, having weak or nonexistent boundaries also means you tend to invest all your time and energy doing what others want you to do or tell you to do.

Never saying no eventually leads to feelings of loss, frustration, and unfulfillment. Without proper boundaries, we tend to confuse our needs and desires with those of people around us. This confusion results in codependency and one-sided relationships.

Hence why it is impossible to enjoy meaningful friendships or romance in healthy relationships without clear personal boundaries. Not only that but when a person does not have an apparent idea of what their limits are, they become subject to heightened stress and intense feelings of hopelessness.

Because they have a penchant for overcommitting to everything and everyone, they often find themselves exhausted and drained of all energy due to how mentally constantly taxing pleasing others is. This either unfolds as burnout or a nervous breakdown, and neither option is ideal.

A lack of personal boundaries also makes a person feel worthless, weak, and never good enough. Then doubt and self-loathing creep in and the ability to voice their truth and communicate their needs verges on the impossible. Therefore, setting healthy boundaries is so important and why it matters so much.

Before you go ahead and blame yourself for yet another aspect of your life that is out of control, take a moment to recognize that your weak and porous boundaries are not entirely a result of your own doing. While it is not your fault that you lack healthy boundaries, it is your responsibility to now developing these self-preserving barriers.

Allow yourself the compassion and understanding that you so readily give to others because you deserve that self-love just as much, if not more than those around you. So why do you suffer from weak boundaries? To answer this question, you need to go far back in the past so you can unearth the roots of these patterns.

As a child, you had little to no control over what your parents, teachers, and other adults taught you. In most cases, those with weak to non-existent boundaries were set a bad illustration of what healthy boundaries are like.

Observing the dysfunctional and codependent dynamic within one's family is a great contributor to this issue, especially when the person is taught repeatedly that love equals what they do and not who they are.

Because the first role models you had, as a child, were your parents and family members, a reflection and close examination of that environment are much overdue. So, consider the following questions to determine whether what you were taught as a child has impacted your views on boundary setting.

- What hints and messages did your siblings, parents, and other authority figures send you when you were a child?

- Were you only shown love and affection when you went along with what your parents wanted you to do?

- Were you only rewarded and praised when you went out of your way, sacrificing your needs and desires for those of someone else's?

- Were you punished and grounded for saying 'no'? Was it the same when you spoke up or talked back?

- Did you feel responsible and compelled to take care of another adult -a parent perhaps?

If your answers are positive, then this is a sign that you were raised thinking that a lack of boundaries and complete obedience are a good thing.

How to Establish Healthy Boundaries

Setting boundaries can be difficult, especially when you have lived all your life accommodating others to the point of neglecting yourself. While there is no one-size-fits-all when it comes to establishing these rules, there are however guidelines you can follow to learn what works best for you in different contexts and with different people. Below are ten comprehensive steps on how you can begin developing strong, clear, and consistent boundaries. So, take the time to examine these measures to determine the best way to implement them in your life.

1.   Understand that Your Thoughts and Feelings are Equally Important to Others

Affirm your worth and value each day, remind yourself of your significance and purpose, repeat this phrase "I am worthy, and my needs are important" until you believe it, and learn to disagree with those who make you think otherwise.

2.   Delineate Your Boundaries

Establishing clear 'no trespassing' lines will allow you to feel more confident about the things you expect in your space, in addition to reducing any misunderstandings or miscommunication with others. So, take the time to identify the boundaries you want to be kept before you move on to implementing them in your daily life.

3.   Identify Why You Need Those Boundaries

Understanding why you need the boundaries you have set to be respected is your motivation to follow through with setting those boundaries. If you do not have a compelling reason, why would you go out of your comfort zone and try to fix certain limits with others or yourself.

4.   Stop Overcommitting

You should not try to please others at your own expense either. When you commit too much to other people and circumstances, this will only generate more anxiety and worries for you.

Not only that but in trying to keep up with all your commitments, you will soon feel burned out and exhausted. This, in turn, will transform into resentment towards others due to how inconsiderate they are. Make a habit of voicing your thoughts and stop overcommitting. Learn to say no to non-essential things like get-togethers, work parties, or other events that are not urgent.

How to Get Others to Respect Your Boundaries

Establishing boundaries is no easy task, especially when you are used to focusing on others to the point of neglecting yourself. Of course, by now, you should be aware of your limits and with what you are comfortable. However, that does not make it any easier to communicate those ideas to others.

It is even harder when those around you have been habituated to you always going along with what they want, accepting their opinions as your own, and always meeting their needs. Now we get to the 'dreaded' part that is, getting others to respect the boundaries you have fixed.

While there is no way to predict the outcome of this situation or how well your loved ones will take your newly established rules, you need to understand that those things are completely out of your control. You cannot expect them to hold your boundaries for you either.

That is nobody's job but your own. For you to have your boundaries respected, you must actively protect them. There is no alternative to this. Picking the right people to hang around with will not absolve you of this responsibility either.

With that said, if you follow the guidelines below, you will have a much easier time not only getting others to respect your boundaries but earning the appreciation and recognition you deserve as well.

- Make your boundaries strong, clear, and persistent

- Communicate your boundaries directly

- Do not let boundary violations slide

The Things to Allow in Your Life

For one, positivity is always welcome. You can never go wrong with positivity in your life. Surround yourself with positive people, better that make you feel comfortable and are always rooting for you, the ones that will be there to cheer you up and make you smile when you are feeling low and need them around. Involve in activities that will help you build an aura of positivity. You can create a safe space for yourself, whatever it is that you feel comfortable with. It can be a room you can run to whenever you at your lowest. Surround the room with things that make you happy: music, pictures, art and collectibles, things that hold good memories and are valuable to you. Totally let go of people that will always bring bad vibes and negative energy into the conversation because you really do not need such in your life.

Another thing you should accept in life is change. You are not the same person you were last year or yesterday. You made a mistake yesterday and have moved on, it is in your past and that does not define you. You must understand that change is okay. You might have different dreams than you did last year, your priorities can change and that is okay you are still discovering yourself and that self-discovery will not end till the day one dies so just accept it and understand that it is part of growth.

Growth is also a concept that you should allow in your life. People grow up and move on, no one wants to remain stagnant forever. Your best friend at a point might have grown and her priorities and ways have change, her vision might not include you again and that does not make her a bad person. You can also outgrow people, you can outgrow emotions, and your dreams can change to something improved. You need to understand that growth is constant in life and at a point, everyone will grow in one way or the other.

Alesia's Journey

I am not sure when, but one day back in 2012, after searching through all my expensive handbags trying to piece together enough money for my upcoming rent payment, I came across a legal pad notebook and I started to write down all my bills, my fears, my goals and more. Once I finished writing, I continued searching the rest of my closet until I became tired, not physically tired but mentally, I was so tired of always coming up short I needed a solution and fast. I picked up the legal pad and my pride and I created a financial budget for myself, there were so many things that I would purchase, knowing damn well I could not afford them. Spending money that I did not have, my motto became "Don't buy it once, if you cannot afford to buy it twice!" I slowly was able to dig myself out of the financial whole I was in. I followed my plan; I was not perfect with it but much better than when I started. I was in denial about who I was and what I had, living my life on champagne dreams with a beer budget. I began to set my heights for something new, something more realistic. By 2013 I could see a huge positive impact on my credit score, less creditors calling my phone, less "money lending" ads in my mail. It finally felt good to "qualify" for something real. Looking back, I wished that I would have taken things such as credit, cash, interest rates etc. more serious, but no worries because as of right now I am proud to look back inside of that legal pad and scratch off each bill that held me back. I no longer spend my money on expensive handbags and cars, I just smile at the fact that I can easily afford them without selling my soul in return. I remain obedient and refuse to live above my means, so at some point you must believe and decide that you deserve better and that setting your standards could save your life. Now if you apply this logic to each area that you struggle with, I believe you can lighten the burden of what is to come. Get your sh*t together early, so you are not wasting important years playing catch up.

11

Raise The Standard

Have you ever wondered why there are so many people in the world who are enjoying lavish lifestyles while there are so many people who are barely scraping by? This is what is referred to as standards and they are important in the path to becoming the best version of yourself. Standards are what you expect of yourself to do and to achieve.

The first thing to understand about standards is that they are a mentality, and it is something that you can build up. No minimum wage worker wakes up one day and sets expectations that they are going to make $20,000 that day.

Now here is something important about personal standards that you need to keep in mind: They are personal. Your personal standards are your own standards, they are what you expect of yourself, and this is important moving forward.

The way you treat others, and you can tell a lot about your standards. This can be viewed in day-to-day interactions and how you expect others to treat you. For instance, if you have lofty standards, then you expect people to treat you with respect. People who have lofty standards will also never stay with a social circle that does not respect them. On the other hand, if you are someone with low standards, then you just go with the flow and never care about how people treat you.

To figure out if you have low or ambitious standards in life, you need to look at three principal areas. The first is your friend circle. How do you expect to be treated, do you expect people to be on time, do you expect people to listen to what you have to say, do people discard your opinion and shove it aside; if so, do you brush it aside.

The second area is with your work life. How do you expect your performance to be for tomorrow, this week, or the next month? People with ambitious standards not only work hard but also expect their performance to be better.

The third area is your future. If you are unsure about your future and cannot imagine a good future, you are happy in? I got unwelcome news for you. But, if you can envision a future, you are happy in and you are currently doing something that will inch you closer to that goal every day, then you have ambitious standards.

Let us be real here, not many people have ambitious standards in every area of their life and there is no shame in that. However, the most important thing is to want to change. First, you must want your standards to change. Your standards reflect your worth as a person, but they can also be used as a metric. Mediocrity is a mindset. No one is born mediocre, and no one is born excellent, we CHOOSE to become mediocre or excellent.

To change your standards, you must look at your own goals and aspirations.

Step One: Face the Truth

The first step of raising your standards is to realize where you are at right now. So, look at the three areas: Social, Work, and Future. Be honest with yourself and do not expect to have higher standards in this phase of assessing where you are. Once you have established benchmarks of where you are at now with your worth as a person, then you can move to the next step.

Step Two: Visualize a Better Tomorrow

Now that you know where you are at, it is time to visualize ahead. So, ask yourself these questions:

- What do I want in life?

- What is my final destiny?

- What do I not want to become?

- What are the qualities I need to develop?

You certainly know already the answer to those questions, and it is time to do work.

Step Three: Plan it Out

You know where you are at now, you know where you want to be, and it is time to know how to get there. Depending on your goals, you are going to need to do work to visualize the plan. If you decide that your standard for earning is higher, then plan out how you will get there. Find out how you can climb higher in the corporate world and learn a valuable skill that pays a lot in today's world. If you want your friends to treat you with respect, then expect nothing but the best from them and do not tolerate any belittling. If they do not respect your lofty standards moving forward, then they were never meant to be in your life in the first place.

Step Four: Set Hard Defined Standards and Metrics

It is particularly important after this assessment that you produce actual standards that you must follow no matter what. It can be a friend, an employee, a father, a wife, or a human being. You might set a standard that every day you will spend at least an hour with your spouse and children, and you will never accept anything less. At work, you might expect to follow certain metrics depending on your work and productivity. Those standards must be high, and you must be consistent with your success in maintaining them.

It can be very tempting to copy someone's standards and we especially like to copy those who are better than us. However, this can be a dangerous thing to do because no one is living your life. Everyone is setting standards for their own living and so should you! While you do not want to set the standards of someone who is miles ahead, you also do not want to look beneath you for comfort. This is a dangerous slippery slope that will end up with you falling off week by week until your standards are gone. Think about this, would Usain Bolt try to race random people on the street? When he wins, would he be happy? No. This is because he is someone with exceedingly lofty standards and even if he is faster than 99.9 percent of humans on earth, he still has ambitious standards for himself which is why he is the fastest in the world.

Areas to Raise Your Standards

Self-care: you must do better in caring for yourself. Most people tend to do the bare minimum when it involves self-care. You need to realize that it is the level of input that you put into your life that will determine your outcome. The better you eat the more you have strength to go through the day, the better you sleep will determine how energized you are the next day, the breaks you take will help you from being stuck on one task without moving forward, the exercise and spa treatments will have an impact in the way your body and muscles feel. Every energy and effort you put into caring for yourself will have an impact in your life, so why not just increase your standards and start to care more for yourself.

Relationships: By relationships, I mean every literal sense of the word: friends, spouse, acquaintances, family, classmates, colleagues, and every other relationship you might have with any person. Low standards for relationships are the reason people keep friends who are more like enemies, friends who cannot be happy about your progress, friends who laugh at you when you are being bullied, telling you it is just a prank or an ordinary joke. Low standards are the reason you go into relationships where you are physically and emotionally abused constantly and cannot leave in fear of your life. Low standards are the reason you suck up to your rich classmates who are bullies and the queen bees of the school, the reason you suck up to that boss or superior at your workplace who constantly takes advantage of you. Raising your standards will help you in attracting healthy relationships that will be mutually beneficial. Raising your standards with relationships will help you attract better people that will surround you with positivity and help you live your life to the fullest in love and happiness.

Aspirations: Do not be afraid to dream big. When it comes to your dreams and goals, never settle for the bare minimum, raise your standards because the sky is your limit. Nothing stops you from being the best in your field with proper motivation and focus, so why will you have low standards concerning the version of 'you' you wish to be. Set ambitious goals for your career and dreams so you can thrive.

Health: Good health is seriously much underrated, extremely underrated. Good health is one extremely asset that cannot be bought with money. Hundreds of rich people are dying daily. Thousands of people regardless of age, gender or status are being rushed to the hospital every blessed day and many of them do not make it out alive. People will kill to be out of the hospital for just a day or even an hour but that is a luxury they cannot afford, so tell me why your health should not be a priority to you. Take care of your health like it means the world to you because it should mean the world to you. When it comes you your healthcare, raise your standards to the peak.

Gianna's Journey

Hello, I am Gianna. My journey here is a bit different, I was the mean girl, growing up I was spoiled so I always got my way. Hanging with girls that I felt were beneath me became second nature, I would choose these ladies because I never saw them as competition, none of them had more than me so it was a win for me, that all changed one day when I became ill, I was diagnosed with Stage 4 metastatic breast cancer before my 40th birthday, I was devastated. My first thought was that no matter what type of "things" I had acquired in life, none of it was enough to buy a negative result. I started to distance myself from people and I realized that no one even noticed, see there was a time that I would only call on people when I wanted to or when they had something for me but at this moment, I wanted people more than ever. I had run off every intimate relationship over the years because I felt they could not treat me as the princess I was, or they simply did not have the "swag" id sought in men. I was lonely as hell; the loneliness was more painful than the cancer honestly. I was so vain, I wanted to keep my diagnosis to myself, but my family made me realize that there was support out there, but that I would need to be vulnerable and show my sincere heart, the heart that I had spent my entire life hiding. I never cared if people liked me because my power made them respect me, in this moment though I just needed a friend and a hug. So, one day after my chemo treatment, I took my head scarf off and pressed the live button on Facebook and I decided to speak from my heart. I apologized for my disgusting behavior throughout the years and promised myself that immature behavior was no longer a part of my life, and that power would now turn into peace. The amount of support I had received was jaw dropping, I have never cried so hard in my life. People were celebrating my life and praying for me even people that had every right to hate me. After 3 years my cancer has spread and each day is a battle, but the blessing I received from changing my behavior has allowed me to love and enjoy each day ahead.

12

Changing Your Behavior

> *"Take a stand against the habit of chaining yourself to your past and your mistakes. Take a stand against people who have purposefully hurt you repeatedly. Take a stand against thoughts and opinions seeking to diminish your worth. They shall not move forward with you. You will not allow them to deny you a new beginning. Make a commitment that their part in your life is finished, you are far too beautiful and far too strong to be a prisoner of things that do not really matter. Reclaim your life!"*
>
> – Dodinsky.

You can gain control of your life by making positive changes to your behavior patterns, so your behaviors support your goals

▶ Write a list of the positive benefits you will receive

▶ Just decide that you are going to do it. Planning is the first step to accomplishment. Until that point, you are just wishing.

▶ Make the new behavior as enjoyable as possible. The more agreeable the new task is to you, the more likely you are to do it.

▶ Control your thoughts. Focus on how you will enjoy the outcomes of the new behavior. Avoid negative thoughts or expectations.

▶ Reward yourself whenever you succeed in performing the new behavior

▶ Each day, measure your progress in adopting the new behavior. This will help solidify the behavior. Changes may take some time, but the results will be worth your perseverance.

Utilize these steps to unlock your greatest potential.

Each tool that you need to become amazing is already placed inside of you. Allow yourself to live and grow each day. Change your mindset, so that you can change your behavior. I believe in you, but it is not enough, if you do not take the time to do the work.

Monique's Journey

It is like everyone knew who I was or at least who I was becoming before I did, once I got into middle school, I found myself being attracted to my teachers, not even kids my age, it was weird. Then in high school, I had a crush on my 9th grade teacher and thought "wait, this is wild" I mean it wasn't the crush that was wild, it was the fact that it was a woman. No one ever talked to me about same sex situations, it was only about boys. But each day, I'd get these butterfly-type feelings when I would see certain women, and it wasn't that I was just attracted to older women, I think that having a crush on them was safe because they were off limits, and I didn't think anyone I hung around would understand what I was feeling, don't get me wrong, there were other gay/lesbian students at my school and they were living their lives out loud, but I was not as sure how my family, friends, and even potential girlfriends would feel. While still thinking that no one knew, I started dressing a bit differently wearing baggy clothing as opposed to the girl clothes that I was forced to wear. I was much more comfortable in gym shorts. I was a basketball player, so I could be myself on the court because I was doing what I loved. But once I got home, I had to be girly or at least try. I was living a double life until one day I just decided to love me enough to be myself and live in my truth. I may not have come out, the way that many others do, but the fact that I knew that there was something giving me these feelings of an attraction. I remember wearing gym shorts under my prom dress, its crazy looking back now because the people that knew me, already knew my sexuality preference. Some treated me differently, and that is okay because when you weigh the amount of love and acceptance received from the rest of the people, it is all good. So, I am not exactly sure what God has for my life, but I am certain that He loves me in a way that allows me to love and accept myself.

13

Accepting You

Self-acceptance is one of the most crucial if not the most crucial step every individual has to take at a particular point in life. Everyone has their demon's and live with it. Most people who like the happiest people in the planet also have their insecurities and dirty secrets. However, those people have gotten to a point of self-acceptance, loving themselves with all they have gotten, letting no flaw or insecurities put them down. If you keep letting your insecurities get the best of you, you would never be able to get yourself together and thrive. When you want to take an especially crucial step, that demon will always arise and make you feel like you cannot do it, or you do not deserve that opportunity to be better and do better for yourself. You will continuously find yourself in a loophole of doubt and self-pity and you might never get to be like those people you truly admire and wish to be like.

At a point, you must realize that if you keep letting this flaw get the best of you, it will not lead you anywhere. Every human on earth, no matter how righteous and perfect they might seem, have all made mistakes at a point in their life. In fact, we humans will keep making mistakes just because we are humans, and no human is perfect. Perfection is a myth, and you should really accept that and stop struggling to attain that. In the struggle to become perfect, you will just find yourself stuck and making more mistakes, never finding that time to just live a little.

Self Esteem

> *"If you do not like something,*
> *change it. If you cannot change it,*
> *change the way you think about it."*
>
> – Mary Engelbreit.

I know of a story of a lady who had a facial deformation since birth. This lady was taunted by everyone in her childhood. She cried herself to sleep every night and even had thoughts of suicide several times. She was a very smart kid but was also bullied by teachers still, saying hurtful things to her like she was possessed, or she was not born of a human. Wherever she showed up, there will always be people there ready to taunt and bully her. This situation made her insecure, and she battled with serious self-esteem issues. She had no self-esteem and was even an easier target for the bullies and haters. She hated the sight of her own face and blamed herself and her parents for her situation though she knew her facial deformation was not anyone's fault. At a point, this lady started to work on her self-esteem. She accepted that the reason she was so insecure and had to confidence in herself was because of her facial deformation which she had no control over. She then realized that there was no point in being miserable over something that she could not control, and she was going to have to live with for her entire life and she knew that she has been through, she knew she did not want to live like that forever. Instead of blaming herself for her insecurities, she accepted it. I might have a facial deformity, but it is not my fault and there is nothing I can do about it. The people who should feel miserable are the ones who think they can make me feel bad about myself because of a condition I was born with. She was able to embrace herself and instead of feeling miserable, running, and hiding whenever she was bullied, she started to feel pity for those bullies, because she now believed that only miserable people will try to make other people miserable to. This new mentality and mindset were able to help her accept her insecurities and build her self-esteem. From someone who could not confidently walk into a classroom without cowering in shame, in fear of people's reaction to her face, she became someone who could confidently walk on the stage and command people's attention.

When you have a healthy self-esteem, you feel good and confident about yourself and your abilities. You know your strengths and limitations and you can work on yourself to become a better version of yourself.

Low self-esteem is not it! With low self-esteem you are weak, when people show you no respect, you just cry and accept it because you feel like you do not actually deserve their respect. You have no trust or confidence in yourself, and it affects you in every area of your life; your relationship with friends and spouses, at your workplace with your colleagues and supervisors, in your social life, in your performance and every other way you can think of.

Just try a little more and be kind to yourself. You would realize that you are doing yourself no favor and only hurting yourself by having zero confidence in yourself.

Loving You

> *"Why should we worry about what others think of us, do we have more confidence in their opinion than we do our own?"*
>
> – Parker Palmer.

There is no better feeling in the world that beats self-love. Self-love is that state where you as an individual have fully embraced yourself, flaws and all and act in ways that are best for you regardless of what other people might feel about you. Self-love is the greatest love. When you love yourself, you do not need to seek validation from other people, you do not beg to be loved or struggle to fit in because you want to be accepted. When you fail to love yourself, how would you expect other people to love you? When you believe that you do not deserve respect, why would you think others will respect you? When you love yourself, your confidence in yourself is extremely high and that aura radiates all around you. At that point, you command love and respect without begging for it. You feel important because you are important and you believe it, you attract good things of life because you feel that you deserve it and that is why self-love is the greatest and most important love. The truth about this is we attract what we believe we deserve. If you believe you do not deserve to be loved and respected for any reason at all then that is exactly what you will get and learn to accept and live with. The way you treat yourself will determine how other people will treat you, but you will keep seeking validation and these things you refuse to give yourself first and somehow magically expect people to give it to you, which will not be possible.

"You yourself, as much as anybody in the entire universe, deserve your love and affection."

– Buddha.

Knowing You

It is often said that self-reflection is the best teacher. When you can reflect on yourself, that means you know yourself so well and recognize your strengths, your limitations, your flaws and even your insecurities, all which helps you work on yourself to become a better version of you. When you know yourself, you know what strengths to tap into, you know your weak points and try to work on them, you can mirror and criticize yourself so perfectly that you know how other people might view you in their own perspective, you understand why some people might have an ill feeling about you and try to work on being a better person. You can predict your actions and reactions and understand the reasons behind them. The better you know yourself will determine how good or bad your relationship with the rest of the world is.

Respecting You

Eleanor Roosevelt once said no one can make you feel inferior without your consent, and I could not agree more. When you respect yourself, that means you realize that you are a person of value and virtue, you realize that you are a person who deserves respect just like every other human and you treat yourself with that mindset, respecting yourself and holding yourself in high esteem, no one can ever make you feel inferior. However, if you do not treat yourself with respect because of one flaw that is weighing you down, you cannot expect or command respect from any other person, because people will treat you exactly the way you treat yourself.

Being You

I am me and not anyone else. I am not that person I watch on the television every day, hoping to be like, I am not that celebrity I keep stalking and emulation, I am not that movie character I love so much, I am not my twin who looks better than me or is richer than me, I am not that sibling who is my parent's favorite child who I've been envious of all my life, I am not anyone else and neither are you. That is a fact and the faster you get to understand that the better it will be. To fully be yourself, there are a few steps to achieve that.

- **Stop Comparing Yourself with Other People:** By comparing yourself with any and every person you encounter, you are doing nothing more than hurting yourself. The fact is that you cannot be better than everybody and you will always definitely meet people who are doing better than you are and have done greater things, greater than you might ever do. Comparing yourself to people will only create hatred in your heart and make you want to do better than every other person.

When you fail to do better than these people, you start to think less of yourself and feel bad about yourself and grow hatred for these people you cannot beat. You believe that it is either you beat them, or they beat you. But life is not a competition. Life does not have to be like that. Life should be taken a step at a time, at your own pace importantly. You do not have to move at someone else's pace. Fingers are not equal and no two people on earth will go on the same journey of life. So why compare yourself with others, why try to do better than everyone else. Why not just focus on yourself instead. Concentrate and look at yourself, not anyone else but yourself. Focus on your dreams and ambition then stand up and work towards achieving those dreams. If you constantly compare yourself to everyone around you, you never might be able to live your own life. You focus on doing better than everyone that you do not even remember what it feels like to enjoy living life. It is very terrifying to live like that and there really is no point in doing that. Just do you.

- **Do Not Try to Live Up to People's Expectations**: Living up to people's expectations is one way to live a miserable life. People will always have something to say, people will always expect you to act or live in certain ways. You cannot fulfill everyone's wishes; you cannot live up to everyone's expectations. If other people want you to achieve certain things, leave them to achieve it by themselves if they so desperately want it, you should concern yourself less with what other people want and focus more on what you want, what you wish to achieve with your life. Set ambitious standards for yourself, think about what you want to do with your life, dream big, be ambitious and get up and achieve those dreams. You cannot let other people decide who you are so always do what is best for you.

- **Be Kind to Yourself**: Relax! Do not push yourself too much. Do not over criticize yourself. You are also trying. Do underestimate your efforts. Moving slowly is also growth, little steps are also steps. If you are not in the same place, you were last year or two years ago, then you have grown and that is really all that matters. Do not be too harsh on yourself because you are not moving as fast as others around you. Everything will fall in place eventually, it might not look that way now, but you will see differences soon, even if it is not much, baby steps.

Emily's Journey

"You're stupid, that idea will never work! You are just wasting your time." These are the things Emily would hear as she gave her friend the exciting details about her new career as a make-up artist. When the friend arrived, Emily could hardly contain her excitement but by the time the friend had left, Emily's confidence seemed to leave out right with her. This was terrible because she had worked so hard training and becoming certified in a field of work that she loved. Emily did not realize that the reason her friend could not be happy for her is because the friend is in a stuck place in her life and cannot seem to find her way out, so it became easy to dim someone else's light to feel good about herself. That afternoon, Emily found herself at a local bookstore and picked up a copy of "Get Your Sh*t Together" and she began to read about people that had nothing to lose and was able to find her confidence, when she would speak to her negative friend, she would simply let her words fly right out the window. Emily also knew she needed to surround herself with people that genuinely wanted to see her win, as Emily continued her social media platform tripled with customers, her services even landed her in the spaces of Hollywood celebrities. So, the criticism that was meant to tear away all that Emily had worked for ended up being used as fuel to light up the world. Emily now has her own cosmetic and facial line of products in stores across America.

14

Dealing with Criticism

Everything is easier with a plan. When you have a plan for how you will deal with criticism, you will be more likely to let it roll off your back when it does not benefit you or take advantage of the advice when it is incredibly helpful. Plus, an effective plan will help you tell the difference! Oftentimes people criticize because of the short comings in their own lives, when people cannot seem to think of anything nice or positive to say they chose negative so they can tear down your self-esteem and your confidence so your life can feel as shitty as theirs. Do not allow those type of people in your personal space because they are wired to suck the life right out of you. Now constructive criticism places a different spin on things, if a person genuinely would love nothing more except to see you win in life, listening to their advice may give you the pinch that you need. You must first know the difference between both criticism and constructive criticism.

Follow this process when you are faced with criticism:

1. To decide what kind of criticism you are dealing with, ask yourself the following questions:

    - What is the source of this criticism? Do they know what they are talking about?

    - What is their intention? Are they truly trying to help me or to hurt me? What do they get out of giving me this criticism?

2. Choose how you want to proceed:

    - STOP. If the source of the criticism is not an expert, avoid giving it any of your attention. The same is true if the person has negative intentions. Just get back to work.

If the criticism is intended to be helpful and comes from someone knowledgeable, proceed with the next item on this list.

3.   Listen intently. The criticism you are receiving could be incredibly valuable.

4.   Clarify. Ask questions. Ensure you fully understand.

5.   Thank the other person. Be appreciative of their efforts.

6.   Process what you heard.

How can you use the information? Decide and apply it.

7.   Return for more feedback. After you have applied your new plan, ask for more advice on how to proceed further. Repeat the process.

Feel free to use your own knowledge and experience to modify this process, but ensure you have a plan to get the most benefits from the good advice you receive.

Jordan's Journey

I am so excited, it has been my lifelong dream to open a coffee shop, not just any coffee shops a coffee shop that caters to the community it thrives in. I want older and younger people to feel good while inside, I want to be able to know my customers daily brew before they even tell me, you know, that kind of feeling. My grandmother drank coffee daily, and some days she would even give us a little taste. MeeMaw, as we called her liked her coffee with a little cream and a lot of sugar. As my cousins and I would play outdoors, I remember telling them that I wanted to be a coffee "maker," I really did not know the correct name for it, but I wanted it. They would just laugh and poke fun at me, some of them would even call me an old lady, but I knew what I wanted to do. Once I grew up, life would start happening and plans became delayed, so instead of my coffee shop I started multiple businesses from stepping out on faith and being determined to win. What I did not know was that my own family would be slow to give the moral support I needed and that hurt. The idea alone that we all played on the same porch, loved on one another, helped one another, even cried together, I just believed that they would be right next to me. But they were not, in fact they would speak negatively, ask me if I were "better" than them, they would barely acknowledge my presence in a room and if they did it was to tease or joke about who I use to be and how could I now be who I am. At first, I found myself dumbing down my accomplishments, I would keep all my hard-earned acknowledgements to myself for fear of one of them feeling less than or inadequate due to my success. I would show up to events that I was not invited to just to show them that I was still who I was back when we were younger, I found myself apologizing for simply being me. That shit felt terrible, I realized that the fact that they did not make it off the porch did not have anything to do with me, we all spoke on our goals and dreams but each of us chose our own path. I have been a pillar of support whole heartedly and I now know that if my support is not reciprocated, I am strong enough to walk alone without remorse. I choose happiness.

15

Survivor's Remorse

Often on the road to success, you will be presented with naysayers – people who have absolutely no interest in seeing you succeed. These people are called "haters," and they will wreak havoc on your progress if you allow them to. Remind yourself that their negativity is a sign that you are doing something right. Please do not ever fall into what I call "survivors' remorse" it is when you have been blessed with the opportunity to become a better version of yourself, while those around you have chosen a different path. People from our old environment tend to make you feel bad about being who you are. They name call, belittle, outcast, and or isolate themselves leading you to believe you have done something wrong or that you have now become "better than them" and we tend to fall for it causing us to downplay your accomplishments, find and focus on our failures instead of our success, they even go as far as to keep reminding both you and others of where you come from in hopes to make you feel bad about yourself. It is all a trap, an emotional trap. What that individual is really saying is "I hate what I have become, I am upset that I did not do more to change my life, I envy the fact that you had enough courage to rise above all of our adversities and press forward, and how dare you make it out of the gutter and into the garden?" As much of a sore spot that this can be, do not allow this energy to win its way into your life. You are enough, and you have done one hell of a job being a great human. Their weight is not yours to carry. Also, know that having your favorite powerful affirmations to draw strength from during these times will help you ward off negativity, even if it is just enough to get you through that moment.

So, how does one go about finding or creating affirmations that work for their intended purpose? Well, it takes a little forethought, but the process is not complicated at all. Regardless of your methods, find an affirmation that touches you – one that makes you want to do it repeatedly, even when you are not facing trouble.

16

Penny for Your Thoughts

Today was the second time I had a conversation about a "penny" and why I appreciate them this week. For those that assumed I was at the top of my game not even 10 years ago, they had no idea that "pennies" saved my life. Saved my son and me from becoming homeless, from repossession, and from the bottom at the time. While he would sleep, I would grab my most expensive handbag and I would place every coin I had collected in the dust bag that my purse came in. I would drop my son off at school and head over to the Coinstar feeling defeated and disappointed because once again, I allowed myself to get to this point. Standing there in anticipation, I noticed that the pennies always outnumbered the silver. And even when the silver ran out, the pennies kept going, without fail, and the amount continued to increase pushing me closer to my goal for the month. I started praying over each penny I found, even when I did not need them anymore. I will pick them up anywhere and anytime.

Strange enough, I prefer them over any other coin. For me it is not about the value, it is about the power behind it. I will forever pick them up and make a wish because I know all too well that I am not above the value of that penny. Its value is immeasurable. I know what it is like to be a penny. I also know what it is like to be picked up. Pennies will always be a big part of my life. They are my anchor, my constant reminder of the vision I have set for myself. Whenever I find a penny and pick it up, I am filled with a renewed sense of direction. Pennies gave me hope and infused my life with meaning when I most needed it.

It does not matter how successful you become; you will always have doubts about one thing or another. Being able to stay positive in the face of adversity is essential, especially when you have a goal in mind. For your benefit, it would serve you to know about the power of a good affirmation and then use what you learn to keep yourself on the right track especially when you face incredible difficulties.

Affirmations let you know that you are doing okay even though you may be feeling as though you are not.

They bring your insights into the forefront of your mind by reminding you of your purpose and worthwhile suppressing negative subconscious thoughts that get in your way. A good affirmation can restructure the way you think if you use it enough.

This practice, in turn, is what keeps you motivated when times get tough. The power of a good affirmation is beyond words, though most useful declarations are just that – a series of powerful words that strike a chord in your mind, body, and soul. The good news is developing an affirmation that works for you is easier than you might think.

Bonus Chapter: The Power of Positive Affirmations

The creation of an affirmation usually comes from experience. You can either do it yourself or learn vicariously through another. Heck, you can even combine the two into a customized declaration that speaks directly to you. The purpose of an affirmation is to help guide you through tough times and negative influence, how the affirmation developed is of little significance.

A little predictability is necessary here, but if you have a clarified vision and a well-organized action plan, you should be able to foresee the major problems that lie ahead before you get to them; this will save you some time and trouble, and it will equip you with the tools you need to succeed despite the inevitable.

The reasons behind the affirmation you create are what matters. The meaning of the words should strike you as valuable and empowering, that way you will want to repeat them all the time. Creating a productive affirmation requires a few things from you:

- *An understanding of who you are at the core of your being*

- *Acceptance of your strengths and weaknesses*

- *An assessment of potential future problems*

- *An openness to grow and adapt*

- *A willingness to take advice from others*

- *Familiarity with your current plight*

- *A resolve to keep working despite the difficulty*

If you consider all those things when searching for the perfect affirmation, you should be able to find one that rings bells in your head. Do not be afraid to change things up a bit if you see an affirmation that is not right. Even if you create your own from scratch, be open to the idea of adapting it to suit your future situations. Overall, you want to develop an affirmation that will speak volumes to your heart and stand the test of time. You can start with the following declarations: "I believe in myself," "I am successful," "I am confident," "I love myself and I am worthy of success."

Powerful Positive Affirmations

- *"Only as high as I reach can I grow.*

- *Only as far as I seek, can I go. Only as deep as I look can I see. Only as much as I dream can I be."* – Unknown

- *"A successful man is one who can lay a firm foundation with the bricks others have thrown at him."* – David Brinkley

- *"I never take advice from someone more messed up than I am."* – Unknown

- *"What you get by achieving your goals is not as important as what you become by achieving your goals."* – Zig Ziglar

- *"I am the star. It is about time I shine."* – Unknown

- *"Use your health, even to the point of wearing it out. That is what it is for. Spend all you have before you die; do not outlive yourself."* – George Bernard Shaw

- *"I am too big a gift to this world to feel self-pity and sadness."* – Unknown

- *"Success is liking yourself, liking what you do, and liking how you do it."* – Maya Angelou

- *"You can't stop the waves, but you can learn how to surf."* – Unknown

- *"If you hear a voice within you saying, "I am not a painter," by all means paint and that voice will be silenced."* – Vincent Van Gogh

- *Do not waste your time in anger, regrets, worries, and grudges. Life is too short to be unhappy."* – Roy T. Bennett

Bonus Chapter: The Power of Positive Affirmations

You might feel like these affirmations do not do anything for you or have any impact on your life, however affirmations can help you in many ways. The only way positive affirmations will be of no use to you is when you struggle with loving yourself and low self-esteem. When you battle with these situations, it is because you are yet to let go of your demons and move on with your life. You do not believe that you are deserving of love or good things of life because of a mistake you might have made or an insecurity with which you are battling. When you say positive affirmations without believing that you are worthy, saying "I am beautiful, and I deserve to be loved" when you have zero confidence in your physical appearance for example will only make you feel worse than you might have been feeling before. The key to making these positive affirmation work for you is to believe that you are worthy, and you deserve every one of these good things. Here are ways these positive affirmations can help you:

- Positive affirmations can help relieve you of the stress and tension you are feeling.

- Affirmations have the power to keep you motivated to do this life thing. Having a bad start to your morning and affirming that "I am going to have a good day, this little incidence will not determine how I am going to spend my day, nothing will kill my joy today because I deserve to have a good day and that is what I will get" this affirmation can help to keep you motivated about how the rest of your day will turn out to be.

- Affirmations give you the power to channel your energy into positivity and growth. It can help you let go of negative thinking patterns into a more positive pattern.

Creating a Vision that Provides Meaning and Direction

Have you ever considered whether your vision is going to provide you with meaning and direction? If you want to reach the top of your game, you are going to have to give yourself a set of tasks that get your motor running. Otherwise, you might fall victim to apathy and laziness, which are the two greatest enemies of success.

In short, defining and creating a unique vision that gives your life meaning and direction is the best way to stay on course for the road ahead of you. This resolution will be the greatest asset in your climb to success. Failing to give your path a definite purpose might eventually result in you not having a path at all.

Personal Vision – 7 Steps to Create a Vision of the Life You Want

Your vision of the way you want your life is just as important as someone else's vision for their life. Moreover, do not allow others to dictate your vision with thoughts or doctrines of things you do not want. Your fate is yours alone; and thus, you should treat it as such when designing your vision for the life you want.

Regardless of what anyone else says, there is no right or wrong answer for your destiny. You are the one who must sleep with it on your conscience at night. However, there are a few steps (*7 to be exact*) you can take to help ensure you are creating an unclouded vision of your life's plan.

- Ask yourself what your life would look like if it were "perfect."

- Write down a list of the things you would like to change in your life today if you could.

- *Talk to your loved ones about their dreams and wishes so that you can incorporate their happiness into your vision if you choose.*

- *Count your blessings as they come, especially the ones that come in disguise – recognizing that they are necessary steps in your quest.*

- *Meditate on your vision to formulate a workable plan with a clear objective.*

- *Consult with a trusted friend or two about insights, ideas, and considerations you may be overlooking or forgetting.*

- *Create visualization boards or other motivational postings so that you can stay focused on your vision throughout the process.*

If you structure your plan around a clarified vision that has a purpose and gives you the direction you will be successful, that is a fact. There are many people who are afraid to move because they do not want to make a mistake. Now that you have your vision you need to know what to do with it so that it does not get squandered on frustration and impatience. Having finesse and practicing acceptance will take you a long way in this game, and it will help you live a life that is free of regret.

The Top 10 Ways to Live a Life Without Regrets

Accept everything about yourself: the

good, the bad, and the ugly

Learn to realize that all phases of life are useful

lessons that you were born to discover.

See the value in the fact that every action you have ever

taken was because you felt justified in that moment.

Understand that everything happens for a reason,

take time to learn from life's lessons, and move.

Discover and respect the great cycle that

encompasses everything in life.

Life will always define those morals

at the forefront of your mind.

Take reasonable chances and accept the

outcome as your fate and walk that path proudly

knowing that you are not a coward.

Never forget that love is stronger than pride; embrace

the power of forgiveness (for yourself and others) and

remember always to give credit where credit is due.

Be fearless, go after your dreams - understand

that anything is possible with enough

passion, persistence, and preparation.

Work in the service of others without

expecting anything in return.

Life is funny in that you can have whatever you want if you work hard enough and stay focused, but if you work too hard and place blinders on your eyes for too long, you could lose everything. The key to life and success is always balance. Live a life that is in line with your unique vision, make it meaningful, and go after it without regret or apology.

You have gained knowledge on how to get your life together by reading the pages of this book. But that is not all you are required to do. Yes, you have gained knowledge, you know what you are meant to do, but there is no one else that will help you get your life together if you fail to stand up and act.

Take a step, small or big steps, anything at all to help you get your life today. You have an instruction manual to help you in this journey of getting your life together. Use it!

I realize taking a step might not be easy, but it is crucial. The first step might be the hardest thing today, but I guarantee that it is the most important. All you really need to do today is to just take that first step into greatness and get your sh*t together.

About Alesia Lester-Braimah

Alesia began her journey to healing as she found herself navigating her new life as a wife and mother of a blended family and adapting to a new culture. She has become both confident and well-versed in what it takes to reach higher. The "Get Your Sh*t Together" concept came about while sitting on the couch scrolling social media and comparing life to those screaming for attention and superficial likes. Sadly, after tearing her life apart by the seams, her daughter Bailey came to show her a self-drawn picture of a butterfly. Alesia, so proud while sitting back, that is at that very moment, it all started to make sense. The life that we are blessed to have does not depend on "likes." It is driven by love, more importantly, unconditional love. Through years of mentoring and speaking, Alesia decided that loving others does not require forgetting about herself. So if that means that she needs to get her sh*t together, that is exactly what she will do. This new chapter of her life is personal.

For coaching services, resources and freebies,

head over to nichecoach.com